The Alchemy of Planes

Amelia Earhart's Life in Verse

poems by

C.L. Nehmer

Finishing Line Press
Georgetown, Kentucky

The Alchemy of Planes

Amelia Earhart's Life in Verse

ACKNOWLEDGMENTS

I wish to thank Sammie and the staff of Purdue University Archives and Special Collections for being the caretakers of the George Palmer Putnam Collection of Amelia Earhart Papers and for allowing me access.

I'm grateful to the team at Schlesinger Library, Radcliffe Institute, Harvard University, for providing the photos of Amelia Earhart used in *Alchemy*.

I would be remiss not to recognize the contribution of my friends in the Waukesha poetry group. Their enthusiasm and feedback were instrumental in shaping this book.

Thank you to Finishing Line Press for publishing new artists and to my editor, Christen Kincaid, for making my book shine.

Love and thanks to my parents, Paul and Jan Ruppel, who knew and believed from the start.

Lastly, for discussing the July 24, 1897 night sky with me, special thanks to Rick at the Astronomical Society of Kansas.

Publisher: Leah Maines
Editor: Christen Kincaid
Author Photos: Cover: C.L. Nehmer
Cover Design: Elizabeth Maines McCleavy
Photos on cover, page 20, and page 35 are courtesy of Schlesinger Library, Radcliffe Institute, Harvard University.

Order online: www.finishinglinepress.com
also available on amazon.com

Author inquiries and mail orders:
Finishing Line Press
P. O. Box 1626
Georgetown, Kentucky 40324
U. S. A.

Table of Contents

To Joe,
who gave me space
to try my wings

preface

*"It is not the names of the men she recalls,
but the alchemy of planes."*

This book was born from a challenge to write a poem about someone I admire. When I workshopped that initial Amelia Earhart poem, my teacher, Margaret Rozga, now the Wisconsin Poet Laureate, told me it was full of ghosts. In other words, I was trying to put too much into one poem.

Recent discoveries have brought Amelia Earhart back into the American consciousness. We marvel at her heroism. We romanticize the mystery of her disappearance. How did a Midwestern girl, born before women could vote, born before the first airplane ever flew, come to be an American icon flying over the hostile waters of the Pacific Ocean? What could we learn if we peeled back the layers of legend and explored the more intimate moments?

Since I had already found that Amelia's story could not be told in one poem, I began at the beginning. We know the ending, but the moments in *Alchemy* are not told through the lens of disappearance. Rather, I concentrated on being in one space at a time, examining each event for its own value, from beginning to end. An extraordinary story unfolded.

Amelia Mary Earhart was born at the home of her grandparents in Atchison, Kansas, on July 24, 1897 (see poem on page 1). She was instantly surrounded by the competing philosophies of her parents and grandparents. Her grandparents, Alfred and Amelia Otis, were traditional, well-off, and respected in their community. In a time when girls were expected to play tea party and wear dresses suitable for playing at becoming mothers, Amelia's mother, Amy, made play clothes for her two daughters—trousers, to be exact. Amelia and her sister, Muriel, learned to shoot guns and play football (2).

Amelia had a vivid imagination and grew up in a home where it was fueled by plenty of reading. She adored her father Edwin, who was a lawyer for the railroad, and shared his love of language. It seemed to Amelia that her father knew everything and could define any word put before him. He once addressed her as "parallelepipedon," which sent his young daughter searching for the dictionary (3). As an adult, Amelia would author numerous non-fiction articles and books. She also wrote poems, submitting some of them to *Poetry* magazine under the pen name Emil A. Harte. The receipt of a rejection slip from the prestigious journal didn't keep her from continuing to write throughout her life.

There's a certain sense of security woven into a child's growing up years when she has absolute faith in her father. But Edwin was far from perfect. He was an alcoholic, and at times, couldn't hold down a job (4). Amelia's childlike trust in her father unraveled over the years as Edwin let her down time and again, eventually squandering his wife's inheritance until the family found themselves in dire straits. They followed the work that Edwin could keep, moving from city to city.

Amelia was a natural leader, making friends and waves wherever she went. She graduated from Chicago's Hyde Park High School in 1915, after having attended five other secondary schools. She then settled in at Ogontz, a finishing school in Pennsylvania.

Over her Christmas break in 1917, Amelia visited Muriel at school in Toronto. There she encountered young veterans hobbling in the streets and was compelled to join the war effort in a meaningful way. She left school, took a first aid course, and became a nurse aide at Spadina Military Hospital in Canada (5).

The first widespread use of airplanes by the military was during World War I, and in 1918, many Canadian pilots trained at Armor Heights Military Airfield in Toronto. Amelia went there to watch the planes come and go, to fuel the spark growing inside her (6).

After the Armistice, Amelia enrolled as a premed student at Columbia University in New York (7). In her book, *The Fun of It*, Earhart recalled, "I think I explored every nook and cranny possible. I have sat in the lap of the gilded statue which decorates the library steps, and I was probably the most frequent visitor on the top of the library dome." (8)

But by 1920, Amelia dropped out of Columbia. Edwin was working hard to beat his addiction and get his law practice back on its feet, and he wanted his girls with him. Amelia and her mother agreed to move in with him in Los Angeles. It was during this period of financial and personal uncertainty that Amelia and her father attended a flying exhibition in California, and she took her first plane ride.

Amelia fell in love with flying and never looked back. On January 31, 1921, she started taking flying lessons from Neta Snook (9). With the help of her family and by working odd jobs, Amelia soon had enough money to buy her own airplane (10). She flourished as a pilot, doggedly pursuing the many firsts set before that original generation of aviators, breaking one record after another.

Though her celebrity grew, the family continued to struggle with setbacks. In 1924, Edwin filed for divorce. Amelia sold her airplane and bought a used roadster, moving her mother from Los Angeles to a new home in Boston. Amelia surprised Amy with a zigzagging tour of national parks en route, including a stop at Crater Lake, which was formed when a volcano erupted, then collapsed on itself (11).

Picking up the pieces again proved to be challenging. A possible solution presented itself in Sam Chapman. Sam was a boarder at the Earhart home for a time. He and Amelia dated and, after her parents' divorce, Sam followed Amelia to Boston. He was an engineer with a good paying job.

But instead of marrying Sam and settling down, Amelia made the unusual choice to take a job. Soon afterwards she moved herself into Denison House, a settlement house where she was employed as a social worker (12). The Boston neighborhood was home to Chinese, Syrian, Italian, Irish, and Jewish immigrants.

By this time, America was consumed with air fever. The whole world watched breathlessly as Charles Lindbergh made his solo flight from New York to Paris on May 21, 1927. Lindbergh was greeted back in New York City with a ticker tape parade (13). The skies surged with possibility. It seemed plausible that flight could be used for more than military reconnaissance and barnstorming. Not only could people now travel quickly by automobile, but the prospect of passenger flight with all its benefits was within reach.

Americans had a taste for adventure. They consumed thrilling tales such as *Skyward,* which detailed the Antarctica expedition of Richard Byrd, and also *We,* Charles Lindbergh's bestselling book. Both were published by G.P. Putnam's Sons.

George Palmer Putnam, known as G.P., began to pursue a crew that would afford him the record-setting flight necessary for his publishing house's next adventure book (14). Attractive, well-spoken and a rising aviation star, Amelia fit the bill. Putnam also recruited pilot Wilmer Stultz and mechanic Louis Gordon.

On June 18, 1928, Stultz and Gordon piloted the first woman passenger, Amelia Earhart, across the Atlantic Ocean by flying a pontoon plane from Newfoundland to Wales (16). Amelia was tasked mainly with keeping the log book, though at one point during the white-knuckle flight, with about an hour's gas left in the tank and the time for reaching Ireland having come and gone, she attempted to take their bearings by dropping a handwritten note from their pontoon plane onto the deck of a passing ship (15). The hope was that the ship's crew would read her request and paint their coordinates on the deck. (Painting arrows or coordinates on rooftops and ship decks, along with following rivers and rails, were common navigational tricks used by early pilots.) The note missed the vessel, landing instead in the turbulent waters of the Atlantic Ocean; a second note met the same watery fate. Still, the *Friendship* crew made the decision to press forward rather than bring their pontoon plane down beside the ship. Ultimately, they prevailed.

Upon landing in Wales, Amelia was besieged by fans and press. She directed credit to Stultz and Gordon, saying she was just a passenger, but the world couldn't get enough of the female flyer. Press and public alike fell in love with the demure aviatrix.

Amelia wasn't the only woman taking to the skies. In 1929, Amelia and her female colleagues founded the Ninety-Nines, an organization of female pilots, still in existence today, so named for the number of charter members (17). They were the female pioneers of the sky.

People often had a hard time looking past a woman's wrapper to her accomplishments. Women struggled to be seen as the capable pilots they were. In fact, Amelia once received an anonymous handwritten note, along with a newspaper clipping bearing her likeness, chastising her for her unruly hair (18).

Amelia continued to buck tradition. She remained wary of marriage, feeling it could tie her down and stunt her career. After a number of refusals, Amelia did agree to marry G.P. on her own terms, making her intentions clear in a letter she presented to him on the morning of their nuptials (19). She would not be locked into a gilded cage, making him promise they would part ways in a year if either was unhappy. The two were married at home by a judge that day, February 7, 1931.

The ambitious newlyweds settled into their new partnership (21). And their marriage did not stunt Amelia's career. In fact, on May 21, 1932, she became the first woman to fly solo across the Atlantic Ocean, making the leap from Harbour Grace, Newfoundland to Derry in Northern Ireland (22).

The pair worked hard and was well-off, though by 1933, the entire country was in the throes of the Great Depression (23). By then, Amelia Earhart and First Lady Eleanor Roosevelt were two of the most recognizable women in the world. They were also friends. One spring evening, after dinner together at the White House, the two women took a night flight over Washington D.C., and then went for a drive in Eleanor's new car (24).

Women were beginning to take the wheel in all sorts of venues. That same summer, two weeks before the annual Bendix trans-continental air derby, officials announced that women would be allowed to take part in the competition for the first time. Amelia became the first woman to complete the perilous race (25). And on January 12, 1935, Amelia became the first person—man or woman—to fly solo over both the Atlantic and Pacific Oceans by crossing from Honolulu, Hawaii to Oakland, California (26).

That autumn, Amelia joined the staff of Purdue University as Career Counselor to Women and an advisor to the aeronautics department. The students found a kindred spirit in Amelia, who lived in the campus dormitory and ate with them in the dining hall. Amelia designed a questionnaire for the female students, asking if they intended to seek employment after college, what their thoughts were about continuing to work after marriage, and how they felt the value of wage earning stacked up against the value of housekeeping (27). She counseled the young women on discrimination, encouraging them to enter what society considered "men's fields," such as engineering. She scandalized the faculty wives by wearing slacks.

It was at Purdue that Amelia found the financial backing to pursue her final aviation dream, an around-the-world flight. G.P. started working on the logistics, and Lockheed Aircraft began building what Amelia referred to as her "flying laboratory" (28).

Leading up to the journey, she spent time unwinding at the California ranch of her friend, Jackie Cochran. Jackie was a cosmetics entrepreneur who would become the first woman pilot to break the sound barrier. The two shared an interest in both flying and mental telepathy (29). (G.P. would reach out to Cochran in the days after Amelia's disappearance to divine her exact location in the South Pacific.)

In the early morning hours of March 20, 1937, Amelia taxied her fuel-heavy Lockheed Electra on the airstrip at Luke Field in Hawaii. Traveling westbound for Howland Island, this would be the first leg of the nearly 29,000-mile journey to circumnavigate the globe at the equator. But as the Electra gained speed, Amelia lost control of the plane, failing to clear the runway (30). The plane was badly damaged and would take weeks to repair.

While Amelia waited that spring of 1937, political tensions ran high. Germany, Italy, and Japan were forming an alliance. Japan was on the verge of attacking China, and the waters of the Pacific were growing increasingly perilous. Amelia was undeterred (31).

Due to changing weather patterns since the original flight plan, she decided to fly east instead of west on her second attempt to circumnavigate the globe. This time, Howland Island to Honolulu would be the final leg of the trip.

She would be making the second attempt with her navigator, Captain Fred Noonan, an accomplished seaman, navigator, and pilot, who had charted commercial routes over the Pacific Ocean for Pan-American. Fred had recently married his second wife, Mary Bea Martinelli, on March 27, 1937 (36).

On May 21, 1937, Amelia and Fred departed Oakland, California. The pair crossed thousands of miles of uncharted jungle, ocean, mountain, and desert, landing and refueling at planned checkpoints around the world. Amelia journaled their adventures, wiring or phoning G.P. from every exotic locale where they landed (32).

The final leg of their trip—Lae, New Guinea to Howland Island, then on to the United States—began on July 2, 1937. Amelia and Fred experienced radio communication difficulties throughout the flight and ran low on gas. The duo disappeared (33). Despite arduous search and rescue efforts and the designation of millions of dollars to the cause, Amelia and Fred have not yet been found (34).

The compelling mystery of their disappearance wasn't the catalyst for this book. It was Amelia, the woman—bucking the role set before her with grit and gumption, always dreaming, never ordinary—who breathed life into that first poem. And when I found I had written a poem with ghosts between its lines, I invited them out of the shadows, and they spread like wind into the pages of *Alchemy*.

Out of bone, a woman.
Up from loam, prongs of wheat.
Into the sky, a longing.

Home Birth, Nearing Midnight

Atchison, Kansas, July 24, 1897

Hot in the belly of summer.
Lightning come and gone, rain
shed into the living fields where crickets
and knob-skinned creatures

make their mid-summer sounds. Edwin
paces the porch, sits, prays, searches the sky
for Cassiopeia, a mother who sacrificed her daughter
to the sea. Over the white house a piece of moon

splinters the sky where Amy labors,
a basin and a ball of string, the Regulator
dutifully letting time take it over,
move through its limbs of metal and wood.

The body like clockwork does what it knows.
An energy ratchets the inner workings,
unfolds itself into a birth cry, a slippery thing
needing thumping and wiping. Amy

meets this intimate stranger, sees the universe
in her open eyes, the allotted moments
already easing by in words and spoons
of porridge and between the lines

of schoolbooks and hopscotch and hem stitches,
fishhooks and frogs in buckets, shoelaces
and all the pedestrian charms mothers and fathers
with daughters do. Amy and Edwin

give their baby a name: Amelia Mary,
after her two grandmothers. Owls
lullaby in the cottonwood. And the face
of lovely Andromeda, who escaped the sea,

turns her starry countenance to the north,
always to the north, toward the star
that brings one back home.

Big Game Hunter

Amy makes trousers for her girls, and now
they hunt big game—tigers, elephants,
and rats, which they shoot
with a twenty-two-caliber rifle. Now

they chase bikes with other bikes,
build stilts from old tin cans. Days are fat
along the Missouri River. There are sandstone caves
to explore, and shells and skulls and spiders

to collect. Then an idea electric—a wonder
they saw at the World's Fair—the girls
collect the tools, begin to cobble blocks and boards.
Soon roller coaster tracks of two by fours

lay shining in the heat before them, stretched
from tool shed roof to ground and greased
with kitchen lard. Meelie goes first,
folds her supple bones into an apple crate,

(already she trusts the economy of one),

and tips herself from roof into air, navigates
the makeshift rails, her repurposed box
barely freighting the twin engines of her legs.
Breathing fast, hair whipping the air behind her,

Amelia slides, lands hard and tumbles,
batters the ground with elbows and knees,
bruises instantly beginning. But it sticks.
Feels like dreams. Feels like flying.

Parallelepipedons and Pancakes

or Word Games with Father

Give me another, please.
Jam. Jam. I'll solve it, Father.
Agglutinative flapjack stack.
A language diagram.

Harsh words hurt my ears.
Lick. Lick. Fingers viscous.
Mysterious words in mind.
The kind for the curious.

A new sled from Dad, longer
than other girls have. Let's not
sit up straight on top. Bellywhop,
into the snow! Like the boys I go.

Pieces for poems in the snow-
covered loam. One more run
before we go home. Equestrians
and pedestrians skirt the base

of the hill where we practice
our navigation skills. Clip clop,
clip clop, carts with horses
don't stop. Safe on my stomach

I slide between hooves, count
my luck. Six legs in view,
but no one is struck.

Edwin Loses His Job

He moves the family to St. Paul,
sets in motion a one-way reel of work,
whiskey, disappointment—the next town
being only a failure away. Once,
he staggers clumsily into the street,
is struck by a car. Once, they wait hours
for Edwin to return home, escort them
to the church Christmas dance: in their best
dresses in their rented rooms, they watch
the loop of their life play itself out
like the frames of a Harold Lloyd movie
(the optimistic everyman hustling toward
prosperity, black and white calamity
unspooling in suspenseful silence).
Amelia unpins the fanciful decorations,
tears up the hand-painted napkins,
turns out the lights, climbs the stairs
to an unfeeling Minnesota night.

                        They say a man
will hang himself if you give him enough rope.
But there are no instructions for a man
dangling from the side of a building, twisting
and trying to climb, no way to tear your eyes
away from the terrible struggle,

                           the inevitable drop.
Amelia will learn to sew. She will learn
to draw and cut patterns from newspaper,
to dye the old silk curtains and sew them
into summer dresses for herself and her sister,
Muriel. She will learn to stay out of the rain.
She will learn to *make do with cheerfulness.*

While Visiting Muriel at School

In Canada, Amelia sees men
hobbling through the streets, empty
tweed where limbs should be.
Knitting sweaters is not enough;
rolling bandages, not enough.

The Great War sees thousands
of Canadian men (together
with the French and British,
Russians, Italians, and Romanians)
taking up the sanctioned savagery.

Toronto's wards fill with blind,
with incomplete, with sick
and traumatized. Her job
is to be merry, scrub floors and carry
trays, to rub the bone-tired backs
and write their letters.

When Spanish flu pushes
like poison gas through the arteries
of the city, it claims thousands.
Amelia stays, ladles out reassurance
and medicine, is struck
with influenza, pneumonia,
a debilitating sinus affliction.

She will never be the same.
No one, will ever be the same.

Soldiers and Planes

War requires bullets and bandages, nurses
and soldiers—scores of young soldiers.

In Canada the romantics fly airplanes, a new
generation of bullets. The planes' kicked up snow

stings the faces of spectators as officers come and go
from the pine-edged field where Amelia observes,

feels a primal call to coax beneath her own
foot the rudder bar that turns the plane, work

in her own hands the stick that drives the nose
up or down, the mechanics of movement

unfolding, blood-wild, through metal and wood
into flesh and bone, so that when, years later, she finally

circles over the California coast, it is not the names
of the men she recalls, but the alchemy of planes.

Alma Mater Statue

Two hat brims bow, nearly
touch in the bronze lap of
Athena—between them
only Browning and a
paper bag of cherries.

An Affinity for Rooftops

Among the stacks of books and bins
of fruit you won't find her. Stables
filled with straw and muck and old men
sitting and thinking and reading and spitting
and places the wind never touches—
the hinges and bedspreads and metal knobs
of bureaus, packets of tea and latches
and kettles and all the oddities of necessity—
cannot contain Amelia.
                              So she climbs.
Climbs the stairs or some rickety scaffold,
grasps the library's gleaming dome
knee over knee over knee until she is poised
upon some cornice or parapet looking down
on whole cities of streetcar wires and silent
moving cars and strangers with prams and shoes
that leave no prints in yesterday's snow, people
getting on with the business of a day.
                              And she peers
from the precipice, where wind blows webs in
and out like lungs, their sure-footed spiders
not retreating into corners, feels herself falling
into each city's bricks and brooms, its merchants
and dispensaries and alleyways with their pungent
vapors that rise, disperse, vanish,
                              and savors
how stories become smaller from above, the sky
bigger even than in Kansas, the great equalizer
of distance erasing every exhausting detail
until there is only the clean line of horizon.

Amelia's First Airplane

The plane is an unbroke horse
bolting smooth across the blue-bellied
sky, its nose, a smooth-skinned beaver
cutting the water home. Amelia
falls in love with the plane she calls

Canary, makes it her own. Makes
of herself an aviatrix in slender jodhpurs
that pillow out over tall and tightly laced
boots, long leather coat, well oiled,
appearing aged from bedding in. And Amelia

and her airplane gallop skyward
on feather-light legs, yellow wings flared
and shining, the one depending upon
the other, the other upon the one—screw
upon synapse, bone upon beam. And when

the fog hangs like traitors
around every tree, the sweet smoke
of roasting corn and potatoes
might rise from the hangar. And
if it is too windy to fly,

Amy will bake a cake; Muriel
bring a basket of sandwiches
for the regulars, who recount
flying the Sierra Pelona,
who have circled the Hollywood Hills,

breathed the same inebriating fumes
of grit and gasoline, who shellac
the eloquent wings and settle the Canary
into her stall, who pat her metal muzzle
and whisper goodnight.

Pilot's Credo

Around the hangar it's
no job, no pay, no fly.
Jobs Amelia will try:
social worker, mail clerk,
delivery truck driver,
designer of clothing
and luggage, telephone
operator, lab tech,
public speaker, English
teacher to immigrants,
mental hospital aide,
photographer, career
counselor, magazine
columnist, commercial
airline pilot, tutor
of trigonometry,
chauffeur, telepathic,
military merry
sunshine, celebrity
spokesperson, poetess,
writer of nonfiction,
exhibition flyer.

Cross Country After Divorce

Between Spokane and the Canadian
border, Amelia and her mother, sun
soaked, pull the used Kissel into Bea's
Blue Plate, any coolness from Crater Lake's
waves having unlaced between Oregon
and Washington, Amelia's foot owning
the gas, pistons pumping out miles between
forests of hemlock and fir, nub to nub,
the way we break each other open with
our inadequacy. This large grief we
carry until our bones become molten.
The mountain opened itself like a world.
The bruised earth covering itself over,
begins again to fill—such careless love.

A Social Worker

Mutton and soap and shit and smoke
and the broken lines of a new language
bleed through the walls
where Amelia comes to teach
the immigrant mothers:

> *Bread, the food we break;*
> *Morning, sun behind buildings;*
> *Daughter, smooth stone in the pocket.*

Families live in stacks above Mr. Ling's
first floor laundry; basketballs slap
the bricks in choppy diction; el trains
and autos speed above and through the streets
of the garment district where she coaches.

> Mr. Sam Chapman has followed Amelia to Boston.
> He has purchased a fine house for them to fill.

From her new room in a south side
settlement house, Amelia makes plans:
gathers teenagers round her mother's hearth
where Amy and Muriel stuff them
with roasted marshmallows and courage.

> Her Kissel, Yellow Peril, navigates
> the ghetto, already filled with children.
> Children piled roughshod in the mohair seats.
> Children pressing their feet against the smooth running boards.
> Children perched like question marks on its bright trunk.

Charles Lindbergh's Solo Flight—New York to Paris

May 21, 1927

Ticker tape saturates
Broadway's unblemished sky
Undulates without ebb
The bright faces of a
Blindly roaring nation

A Publisher's Dream

She must be well spoken,
college educated, young and poised.
She must have aviation training,
be daring and attractive.

George assembles a team, and pays them well.
Only Amelia (as the first woman to cross
the Atlantic by flight) will not be paid. But
she senses the significance of the opportunity.

While the men prepare the plane, the finances, the pilot,

Amelia attends the theatre with George's wife.
Amelia swims in the ocean with George's sons.
Amelia writes a will and watches for hours,
their pontoon plane, heaving amiably at its moorings.

Oranges

What to do if a destination
should have been reached, but still,
there's no land on the horizon:

fly low over a passing ship;

write a note to the ship's captain,
asking him to have his crew
paint their bearings on the deck;

put said note into a bag with
a couple of oranges for ballast;

take careful aim
from the plane's hatch and drop
the weighted sack;

pray it reaches the ship's deck.

A Nun from Newfoundland
June 18, 1928

On the Eastern tip, the men of the *Friendship*
repair the seaplane, wait for the weather to clear.

Amelia goes to the Catholic school for maps,
but finding only a large globe,

abandons the pursuit and promises
to write the Sister if they hit land anywhere,

so that when through the wool of wet and fog
a flock of fishing vessels swims forth

into their plane's shrouded field of vision,
the carry-on pilot

is already composing, already considering
how she might attempt to cross alone.

The Ninety-Nines

Why do you have to fly?
   Airplane threading the sky,
   an untethered needle.
   Cabbage moth wings at the
   screen, bluestem horizon.

But aren't you frightened, ma'am?
   Seals breathe at the surface,
   a vulnerable plane.
   Shard from a child's finger.
   Doe in a fast current.

Does your household suffer?
   Maple trees flourish in
   season, kettles keep. Oil
   to a hinge. Jetsam, clothes
   pin, maternal fulcrum.

Unsolicited Tip

Dear Amelia Earhart,

You look quite like a cave
woman in this photo
from yesterday's paper.
Won't you please comb your hair
and try to look a bit
more civilized next time?

Truly,
Anonymous

Marrying George

A.E. to G.P., February 7, 1931

I ask not
the whole of you,
the untamable
inside well of you,
nor shall I gift
to you
the whole of me.

I require
no archaic faithfulness,
only honesty,
and promise the same
to you.

Should this union
trespass untethered
into the crux,
I keep for myself
a shelter,

and offer
from the wide river of heart,
that familiar basin
where the tempest of you
reverberates
across the pressed place.

Amelia Earhart and George Palmer Putnam

(Photo courtesy of Schlesinger Library, Radcliffe Institute, Harvard University.)

Settled

Putnam Family Home, Rye, New York

Mother sends the silver. A.E.'s hats and heirloom quilts exhale
    into G.P.'s suits and Inuit arrowheads. Her fingers scale the ivories,
hatch crocus and tomatoes in the sandy soil,
    notes and seedpods spooning over Long Island Sound,
parachuting gracefully toward the surface.

The polished pair swims or sails or rides horseback among the birch
    and low-hanging boughs jammed with black cherries. A world
away from their Manhattan apartment, they awake
    to eggs and bacon, orange juice and ink from the ribs of newspaper
she folds down to inquire: "Would you mind if I flew the Atlantic?"

The Gallaghers of Derry

May 21, 1932

Mr. Gallagher's cattle feel it first—
a red buzzing that cracks open the sky,
a great shadow gliding across their hides
like a ghost. It brings the children
running. The farmhands, too, are curious,
first to greet the curly-haired woman
all streaked with gasoline and go get it

come from America,
come from America, alone,

inquiring of the nearest line
to telephone her husband.

Mrs. Gallagher prepares a stew,
lays out clothing, fresh sheets,
demands nothing of this sensible
stranger, only wonders at how she came,
through the banshee storm of lightning, the ceiling
of low-hanging fog, to be vested
in Ireland's rolling green.

Celebrity Credo

Set a record and then
make the lecture circuit,

set a record and then
make the lecture circuit,

set a record and then
make the lecture circuit.

Amelia and Eleanor Start a Conversation

Probably, in the cockpit, they don't discuss
the falling price of pigs, but the white gloves
of stars pressing the cockpit window.

And when the two drive the boroughs of D.C.
in Eleanor's roadster, they likely don't discuss
the city's migrant homelost,

but the heeled foot on the pedal, the wind,
the warmly lit dwellings where husbands are stoking fires
and housewives are storing up their dreams.

Where a woman stands before her looking glass
to remove an earring, a man lifts a hat. One
unbuckles a shoe, lets it drop off the toes, inches down

(a parcel at a time) a sleeve, a stocking, a skirt,
until their asymmetry is apparent, until the bared beauty
of sameness appears ungirdled before them.

Women Fliers Compete

A man wins only for
himself; his sister wins
for the sorority.

Hawaii to California

January 12, 1935

She calls them cowards—
crows that caw about danger,
about cost—and prepares
to cross another ocean.

She takes long walks
on the beaches of Waikiki.
She feathers her nest
with dogma. Alone

over open water, the pushing
waves of critics' wingbeats
persist. Rain, stars, fog, fumes,
and the welcome visit of voices,

two-way, from radio stations
and ships—G.P., clear and crisp.
After 18 hours, A.E. disembarks
into the open arms of thousands.

Incoming

Why did I choose college?
　　Rain gives itself into
　　river, river into
　　sky. Intellectual
　　dowry, interest, hope chest,
　　domestic dividends.

Will I seek employment?
　　Abandoned, young turtles
　　follow sun, nest to sea—
　　hard-shelled delicacy.
　　Unused asset. Powder,
　　pillowcases, pin curls.

What advice did she give?
　　Undisturbed, honeycomb
　　forms a winter's amber
　　feast. Private contentment,
　　coupling at ease; follow
　　your visceral compass.

At a Factory in Burbank, 1936

The metal comes to Lockheed
by locomotive, a train that spills steam
from its hot orange heart,
brings the grist for a flying lab.

Tinkers mold the metal, rivet a fuselage, the silver
wings that demarcate the age of aluminum
from plywood, air traffic control
from a panorama pocked with painted arrows
on rooftops and ship decks.

Columnists weigh the boundaries
of the human spirit against the cost
of public confidence, of search and recovery.
Amelia advocates safe flight for all.
Amelia has always advocated.

Mechanics retrofit her airplane, remove
cabin windows and crowd the customer cavern
with fuel tanks, polishing the body
of A.E.'s Electra Model 10
into a super-charged airship.

And in the lit heart of it, gunning
for around-the-world adventure,
the crackerjack with her rucksack,
leather skullcap, thermos of tomato juice.

Postcards and Premonitions

bowl of moon
coyote call
disquiet palm

Before her morning orange juice, Amelia autographs ten envelopes
to be postmarked at cities along her round-the-world flight. Upon
her successful return, they'll sell the collector keepsakes at Gimbel's
department store. So before her fork touches her eggs, she signs
an additional fifteen. And before getting into bed each night, Amelia
pens twenty-five more cargo into the weighted heart.

muscled flank
fast ride
doubt to the wind

An Attempt at Howland, From the East

March 20, 1937

Amelia taxis the Electra, acquiring
        speed, and the right wing dips.
    She throttles down the left engine,
  turning the plane left, straining
            the landing gear, which collapses,
        first the right side,
            then the left.
Robbed of its wheels, her aircraft skids
        (metal pealing away
    in a searing river of spark and sound)
  to a stop in its own gasoline,
            puddling fast
    onto the wounded
        runway.

Her plane is shipped to Lockheed
        in pieces, its belly sheared
    and burned, spirit bruised.
  George reaches out to ships
            of personnel already in place
    to track and assist his wife,
            secures donations
for repair, renews government clearances
    at every exotic locale
  where landing strips
have been laid down, pushes out
        rounds of book tours
    and lectures, holds back
        the insatiable crush.

Killing Time

Spring, 1937

I
Japanese raptors hedge southward,
hunt raw meat resources for a hungry
Empire. The razor beak of their ambition
panics the people of the Pacific.

II
While attempting to land, TWA flight 15A,
wings weighted with ice, spirals
nose first into a gully in Pennsylvania,
killing all 13 passengers onboard.

III
A woman's clock keeps pace
with her strides—the cords of blood—
puts away the thing she desires as peers
pass into motherhood, the role required.

IV
Thirty-six flame to their deaths
on a Jersey docking field. From the charred
skeleton of the Nazi zeppelin *Hindenburg,*
only specters rise, stunned.

V
Friends fallen over water find no mercy
in nature's cruel oceans, her granite clefts,
no milky ashes left for archive. Many do less
and perish, a saltcellar collection of dreams.

VI
Shards of metal pulverized beneath
the pestle of A.E.'s burning fuselage
still gleam like mirrors, stick in the craw
of Hawaii's Luke Field Runway.

Amelia receives an advance and works
on her next book, *World Flight.*

A Shining Adventure

Amelia collects pictures in her mind,
observations in her journal pages:
thick groves of oranges in the panhandle,
rice fields outside Suriname, rain forests,
ships in the doldrums and river deltas,
rainy season in the desert, dunes and
seaside villages and mosques, huts made of
mud and grass for a thatched roof, tribesmen who
sit and think and spit, and the crowded slums
of Calcutta, its narrow alleyways,
bazaars and markets and exhaustion, so
tired. They land in Lae, New Guinea to rest,
refuel for the last leg of their journey. Fred
drinks; Amelia wires G.P., almost home.

An Attempt at Howland, From the West

July 2, 1937

Her mind is a thousand boxes;
she opens them one at a time.

Into the labyrinth of the Pacific,
the Electra's clockwork ticks out

the time   waves of static   rock
the cabin   fill the shells of her ears

tearing open the lid   she pulls fear
out by its craw   demands a look

into its liquid eyes   points
her windshield   toward it   gravity

doing   what it knows   forcing
the hapless   tides

Amy

We don't teach our children to jump; they are born
with an instinct for flight. Our arms are ready when they first leap
with all the wonder a body can hold. Before you were born, I lost
a baby I knew only by the flutter of his heart inside my womb.
We had only the moments of dreaming what his life would be.
Before you were born, I dreamed of you, of what our lives would be,
the things I would teach you—how to braid your shoelaces and knot your hair,
how to make bread and buttonholes, how to take the train to St. Louis, our bodies
humming in time with the clacking wheels, how to get up, get up and grip
a challenge by the collar. Today the butcher asked after you and I searched
for the words, but there is only a hole in my mind where questions
circle and circle, a picture show in my head, a constant
unquiet. Awake nightmare, this stone of grief,
of not knowing, clutched in the knuckles of my brain. The mind
doesn't let go, but keeps what if in a bag by the door
along with cold cream and a scissors, a change of clothing.
The moon over you is the moon over me is one moon,
willing the tide to move, this mother to hope.

Amelia Earhart with her mother

(Photo courtesy of Schlesinger Library, Radcliffe Institute, Harvard University.)

fred's wife

eats an egg with toast
calls the cat in from the yard
burns the lamp all night

Moon

What is it that comes to the edge
of the water with its inhibition hushed,
sees the side not visible, the beautiful
trees, a wide warm, this unbroken land.
Sea spine. The impossible crush.
Sunken maze. Moon pull. Limestone
skeletons in low tide. Boat bound.
Light in slices. What unbecoming,
the mottled mission. The night lagoons
of their eyes, these cracking creatures.
Look up toward the lucid stars. Planet
pooled. And the moon—sky fossil.
Secret keeper. The eyelid of morning
closes over its orb, these old ghosts.

Finding Amelia

I expect to be overwhelmed by Poseidon's net
of parallels and meridians, but my feet
are gravitized beneath the table. I peruse
the boxes, find the pencil scratchings
where her hands scrawled to-do lists on tablet
paper, a poem on a scrap of newspaper.

With white-gloved hands a librarian unwraps
the suede jacket, and I imagine the vamp of naked
metal and thrust lifting Amelia in that jacket
into a universe laid out in stars and angles,
her brilliant stem burning in the altitude.

But the jacket lays in an acid-free, lignin-free box,
its only remarkable qualities being the label
and the knowing (Abercrombie and Fitch,
and how it leaned on her vertebrae, warming).

Woman. Pioneer. Wife. Enigma. We ride
her legend until the rivets bulge and we are lost
in the waves of her infinite equator, with only

a shaft of bone and a blade of severed glass,
a curve of shoe rubber in the sand for compass.

Bibliography

"Amelia and Eleanor Go for a Ride: Based on a True Story." C-Span 2 Book TV. Introduction by Jewell Stoddard of Politics and Prose Bookstore in Washington D.C., presentation by illustrator Brian Selznick, 2 November 1999, https://www.c-span.org/video/?153317-1/amelia-eleanor-ride.

"Amelia Earhart Landed in a Field in Ballyarnet in Derry on May 21 of 1932." YouTube, uploaded by Amelia Earhart Legacy Association, 21 March 2017, https://www.youtube.com/watch?v=t7PHJ9jPwRA.

"Amelia Earhart's Lockheed Electra 10E Special NR16020." This Day in Aviation, 1 June 2018, https://www.thisdayinaviation.com/amelia-earharts-lockheed-electra-10e-special-nr16020/.

Burden, Shirley C., dir. *Look to Lockheed for Leadership*. 1940; Burbank, California: Lockheed Aircraft Corporation. Film.

Earhart, Amelia. *20 Hrs., 40 Min.: Our Flight in the Friendship*. 1928. Washington D.C.: National Geographic Society, 2003.

—. The Fun of It. 1932. Chicago: Academy Chicago Publishers, 1977.

The International Group for Historic Aircraft Recovery. *The Earhart Project*. Retrieved June 25, 2019 from https://tighar.org/Projects/Earhart/Archives/Archivessubject.html

Ryan, Pam Munoz. *Amelia and Eleanor Go for a Ride*. New York: Scholastic, 1999.

Stone, Tanya Lee. *Amelia Earhart: A Photographic Story of a Life*. New York: DK Publishing, 2007.

Wels, Susan. *Amelia Earhart: The Thrill of It*. Philadelphia: Running Press Book Publishers, 2009.

"When Amelia Earhart Landed in a Derry Field." BBC, 31 May 2015, https://www.bbc.com/news/uk-northern-ireland-32934928.

Winters, Kathleen C. *Amelia Earhart: The Turbulent Life of an American Icon.* New York: Palgrave Macmillan, 2010.

Colleen Nehmer and her husband, Joe, at Purdue University. The sculpture of Amelia Earhart is a duplicate of one made by artist Ernest Shelton in 1969.

C.L. Nehmer has been a copywriter, bookseller, medical assistant, barista, and school librarian. Her work has appeared in *Southern Poetry Review, Pedestal Magazine, Bacopa Literary Review, Southword, Sunlight Press* and *An Ariel Anthology 2018*. She was a 2019 Best of the Net nominee for her poem "The Electrician's Office." Her poems have earned prizes from the Wisconsin Fellowship of Poets, including the Kay Saunders Memorial Emerging Poet Prize.

Colleen grew up watching the boys build and run model trains, cars, and airplanes. In elementary school, she wrote a paper about two brothers who invented an airplane in their bicycle shop. From the field behind her childhood home, she observed the jets that crisscrossed the sky above her, wondering what exotic destinations were in store for the passengers. Black and whites of a disappearing aviatrix captivated her to be sure, but they were only the glossy cover of Amelia's story. Colleen fell in love with Amelia's brand of feminism later in life: business savvy ahead of her time, advocate for women, guts beyond measure, love on her own terms—all of it in a man's world.

With every flight she takes, Colleen still marvels at the sensation of levity and the mechanical miracle of hanging in the sky. *Alchemy* is her debut book.